no cage contains a stare that well

matt robinson

Also by matt robinson

BOOKS

A Ruckus of Awkward Stacking (Insomniac Press, 2000)
how we play at it: a list (ECW Press, 2002)

CHAPBOOKS

tracery & interplay (Frog Hollow Press, 2004)

no cage contains a stare that well

matt robinson

MISFIT

ECW PRESS

Published by ECW PRESS 2120 Queen Street East, Suite 200, Toronto, Ontario, Canada M4E 1E2

NATIONAL LIBRARY OF CANADA CATALOGUING IN PUBLICATION

Robinson, Matt, 1974–
No cage contains a stare that well / Matt Robinson.
Poems.
"A misFit book".
ISBN 1-55022-711-4
1. Hockey--Poetry. 1. Title.
PS8585.035172N6 2005   C811'.6   C2005-904295-8

Editor: Michael Holmes/a misFit book
Cover and Text Design: Darren Holmes
Typesetting: Mary Bowness
Printing: Marc Veilleux Imprimeur
This book is set in Goudy and Americana

The publication of *no cage contains a stare that well* has been generously supported by the Canada Council, the Ontario Arts Council, the Ontario Media Development Corporation, and the Government of Canada through the Book Publishing Industry Development Program.
Canadä

DISTRIBUTION
CANADA: Jaguar Book Group, 100 Armstrong Avenue, Georgetown, ON, L7G 5S4

PRINTED AND BOUND IN CANADA

ECW PRESS
ecwpress.com

Contents

for the teams and the players;
for my dad and his Saturday mornings spent;
for my grandfather and his Halifax Blues;
for Marissa

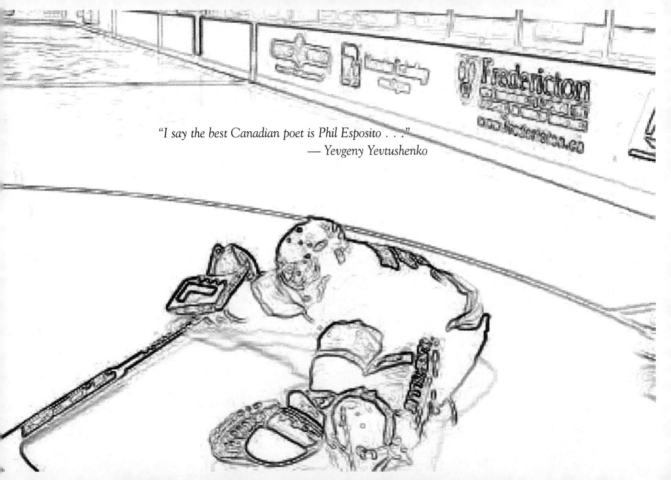

"I say the best Canadian poet is Phil Esposito . . ."
— Yevgeny Yevtushenko

how we keep it together

        borrowed tape. the last bits that barely hold, the cardboard
hollow coming off in our hands and ending like most

of our endings: badly, non-functional, a surprise. never enough. or,

        old laces; a reinvention of what we've already had used
and broken. we pull (and hold) up our socks in

this way; tie things off: a fine-wristed line between tourniquet

        and noose.   scrounging: pennies, or dimes in a pinch. a
penknife or flashed tip of some other guy's lighter. when

the ends start to unravel, you burn. a crucible effect.

        — extremity as closure, as a way of bringing things back.

zamboni driver's lament

                       i know hate, its line-
mates. believe me. your kids have, i'm sure,
wasted — all early morning anxious
and weak ankled — their first impatient
shuffle-kicks and curses on me. no cage
contains a stare that well.   and despite
my perch, i too know damage: precise,
zeroed-in maps of possession and loss, traceries
step-chiselled into moments that loop
around and into — through and across —
each, the other.   because i am always,
when push comes to shove, behind glass
— seated, and away — i've become a fan of
jealousy, can pick him out in the looping
confusion of warm-up. i have his sweater
hanging somewhere on my wall.   indulge
me.   tell me: can you understand what it is

to be something most others only wait,
grudgingly, through; endure?   i can and
do, can and do.   i am a common
cold, the advertisements that linger too long
before a feature.   and though you
may never see this, the lights — i can assure
you — go down each night; the scoreboard's
bulbs snap and flicker, then die. but the ice,
it seems, will always be there: a constant wound
to dress, a scar i run myself along.

why we wrap our wrists the same each time

you'll do anything to beat it, the scoreboard clockishly
familiar script: this sophomore jinx.   that much, you
know.   nothing is beyond you and your sweat-desperate,

wet-dog's shaking nonsense — that furious denial of what it is
you've leapt the boards for and charged willingly right
into.   most anything, for sure.   you'll stop, for instance,

shaving: till your chin's as shift-end ragged as your sleepless breath
at night; start, again — your hand and blade an intermission's
echoes, stale and old glove-hollow with what they hold.

you'll sleep, too, with all these women on the road —
their tired, pooling eyes so many pairs of tinted lenses: shading you
from the glint-glare edges of each next game's anxious

puckdrop.   (your wife? at home. or, out with the girls, her
sisters even — to catch a movie, grab a bite. but you've been
married near three years now, and there's no curse, no hex

in that arena, till the seventh.)   so: it will continue.
          you'll lug your anxious trying and denials, a sack of pucks:
onto the ice and back again each night, a cool black weight, a

mustiness always hanging in the air.   you'll purse your lips
and breathe deeply through your nose.   and with each shift's
frantic convincing, you'll simply grow more sure — damn near,

at times, indignant — that you will, in fact, do anything.
          you know that now; know the only question left is: *when?*
          it's this you carry with you; a faulty strap about to snap its

last just as you push off from the post or skip-step the bench
door's gullied threshold and scar hard into that first stride's cut
of ice.   but right now your hotel room's phone is ringing,

its message light sore red and blinking out the score.   and
even as you segue sore-ankled and unsteady from the shower,
you know you'll reach a bit too roughly for the cord, clutch at it:

the one last loop of tape that tugs your wrist too tight; that
numbs your hands, cuts to the quick.   that much, you know.

puck triptych

a pitched understanding of something past.   or, that fear we hope to face
head-on until it slap-tacks the chest and then flutter-aches down to our feet,
where it stalls and spins, coinish: an obedient bruise we chance, and trip over.

perhaps: the pupil? its glared hollow (at those fierce, fatigued moments when
it seems our joints spit nothing but adrenal curses — hiss feral at the question
of anything more in the face of it).   or anger as light; perhaps, even, its inverse.

even: a small dark speculation.   afternoon shinny. how i nearly trip-chiselled
that boy a new eye: a smelt fishing hole through the pond-smooth sheet of his cheek.
my stomach's pit, turning back, cold and hard with the fresh blush catch of the ice.

to montreal, by bus, for the game

                        there was the moment: racked
long and rigid, extended slow-frame cinematic between

the widening eyes' competing vices, stretched rubberband's
near-limit taut, of the rain. all of — a sea now

un-parted after years — a sudden. the instant biblical,
or near. the sky a headlong torrent tear; like

what we imagine must be the theatrical
interior of a drain just after a plug's grudging acquiescence;

a science of singular purpose, direction. (this is what proximity does
to proportion: explodes it.) and our telling? we hadn't yet

been drinking, so when the highway uncurtained — stepped
out of the rain, smoothed the now drying lines

of its travel suit's legs to their former slick grey fabric weave
again — we simply turned walkmans up one notch

further, turned away from both the streaking
windows and each other, dove into the crisp assurance of our

magazines and papers, drowning out the possibility
of conversation. we tried to deafen the crashing and thrum

of the water in our ears; wished we could roll the windows
down and drink the air: gulp it loud until it

parched, until it cracked the hollow gulleys of our throats down
to our lungs. left us spilt, and split.

house league photo

                          recollection is not a faded black-and-white
snapshot, no bruised paper's sepia-stained insistence —

i'm not old enough for that. coloured, hued and hewn,
it is instead a commotion of smells and sounds, and a strained ciphering

of the shapes, their chill crystal geometry, through something akin to
morning-breath fog on hockey rink glass.

                                in fact, the lapses,
the inaccuracies, are in themselves a reminiscence: a frustration

not unlike the anxious zamboni moments between that last lace or
chinstrap and the first cut of ice.

                         and so this process
of memory, of revisiting ourselves, becomes that musty rubber shuffle

down a blade-scarred mat from locker room to cool,
hard motion.

　　　　　so even these pictures, their cardboard frames now
just as ragtag as our mismatched, ripped knee socks, are not

as concrete for me (though actually here in hand) as the salt-sweat,
leather-rot staleness of the gear, the waft-curling

smell of rothman's smoke on my father's breath, or the dull thuds: of pucks
on the dead dashers of boards, of early saturday morning trunks.

handshakes

                game's done.   and the scoreboard's
wrong-enders — the losers, put plain and simple —
stumble their way towards the centre circle

        to concede.   their hands less purposeful now; a limp collection

of weathered flags in the stark, still windless
day that is the end of overtime.   the end of overtime,
that is, for those whose gloves and sticks haven't

        fireworked themselves into the shouting air's cascade of

eventual debris.   they are a glum recessional, these others:
the conductors of the darker, slack-necked
music of a sudden loss.   they cue — it seems —

        the done-with-disbelieving crowd: that symphony

of defeat, that drum-brushed low rustle of so many feet and
their shuffle towards the exits.　　　　but, without fail,
they still offer their stilted hands.　　　　a final act — this is conclusion,

　　　mimed.　　　　　and some — take that hands-in-pockets gentleman

up in the mezzanine who lingers just a stride too long; some recognize this
for what it is: the fatigued sign language of want; a flaccid
gesture towards everything he knows he'll now never, ever have.　　　and

　　　they certainly know all this — the players — and they wish

　　　it wasn't true.

　　　they wish:

uncertainty as a stance, among other things

for those few there is the way a rebound is
                    like memory: an urgency of legs

and colours and motion all shrouded in
                    a fine cooling mist. a goalmouth scramble

recollection, it is a kinetic echo; near
                    arbitrary, but dependent upon, among other

things, the slow melt of ice in front
                    of a crowd and the strength of ash

or steel. the physics of it, while somewhat reducible,
                    always open to circumstance, to the chance

deflection of another's passing by. and, the fact is,
                    we only think we understand

shear force.   heedlessly seeking something other than
the fluid purgatory of movement,

it weaves and appears — a shining and black
immediacy — long enough only to impart

a glancing blow.   and afterwards, you are left, prone;
heavy with the effort and

your protections; all awkward anticipation and cautious
backward glance. meanwhile, the ice —

a frozen stolid water clock — shifts unaware between its states:
between hard scarring and slick healing.

the same as it always has.

the same as it always will.

tracery, interplay

each successive autumn, everything you've grown unsure of trundled to
your local rink and unzipped; the fragrant bloom of that.

     an empty rink: a rumour. night's end, all we're left
with. the steel-stepped scholia of each other's attempts. suggestions, all.

*

a broken stride's not, necessarily, a distinct kicking motion — though the results are often the same, often called into question.

       overtime? a throat blood-ready to roar, or be slit by quick-shouldered motion, by a mis-turned blade's glancing edge.

           *

the television won't scream back, can't be goaded into anything
rash. so: just one more *keith's*, then.   initiate, don't retaliate.

     and morning after, the throat's a pond zambonied with steel
wool; ribbed and rucked harsh with breath after breath, after.

*

cycling, they work the boards near thin

                                   we've paid good money for these
seats, we tell ourselves, and this — well, this is
the payoff.   almost.
            the thumb and forefinger near itch
with it.   and they tussle, here,
sweatered in the corner; popcorn spills, front
row, onto beer-insulated laps.   periods stall. end.
            and we try to speak to each other
in knowing tones about what we've seen
so close.   but to call it — to make some nodding
reference to — *trench warfare* is a dis-service to
both, their vital strains. they churn, but:
to metaphorisize this loosely is a flaccid, flagging
violence.   a slack-skinned, clumsy chuckle
of an idea; a pen sprung and cracking ink
every which way. only
a cruel nonsense and its stain.   *better then*, we think: of sex.

a mimed intercourse. men, their arms
strobe-splayed against a breathy sheet of
glass.　　　　a blink's intaglio.　　　　then kicking away and
into each other.　　　　*agitprop?* we venture, weakly.
　　　　and we try this way, near apoplectic
with our effort, to sing hoarse and throaty
over the crowd, to herald loud and new of this perimetric
show.　　　　but, perhaps,
to simply take it for what it is, to fail
to make something other from or of it, might not be wrong.
　　　　sometimes a coupling is only coupling — the air
not a heavy wet blanket, but simply breath after breath
after breath.　　　　a lexicon can be matter — as it turns
out — of fact, and still enough.　　　　our hands
are slick with nothing but what passes
for buttered topping. and, yes, we taste salt when we lick
the film off of our teeth.　　　　we are here, in

the front row: a team is losing, a team is winning.
or, the teams, perhaps, are tied.   there is a score and
we can see it glow, bold red, above our heads if only sitting
back a bit and relaxing our hunched shoulders.
                    these seats, our lowered bodies
begin to tell us, *are all too real, are somewhat unforgiving.*

best cut so it rests just below the chin

1.   statistics — the backs of those
o-pee-chees — be damned. there's much to be said
for the dead, for our casualties
of practice.   the morning paper
(with its abbreviation & long-division
wisdom) would be well served by a behind-the-bench alcove
visit.

2.   ash. breath after
a loss, steady and bark dry, rustling. an understatement;
a veteran's curve — a slow-arced subtlety
of years: of power plays, time pinched
with the farm team down in some
                          main street-splintered town.
          the balance of ice and acetylene; a backhanded
recognition.   then, a rookie
sensationouttajuniorflash: the brash collision
of function and style: of fibreglass overlay
and a half-shield smile.

3.   we end.
but, tunnelled back here, reincarnation's to be
had, near free: a quick hand
and a steeled shift-sprint to the street.
          just add canadian tire: then saturday night
becomes saturday morning, again.

splinter

there; he's almost done — with the cleaning.   the emptying of this
godforsaken basement, its grey-walled catacomb for everything

this bloody family has ever owned and then, at some point, tired of.   and

he likes this: his coldroom now finally, nearly nothing: just a sparse autumnal
leaf-spray of past-their-prime paint chips and newly empty space; a crisp,

cellared void, save for this kindling sprawl — the still-spilled hedgethickish racket

of his last boy's old splintered goal sticks.   they're *moving soon,* he'll tell his son:
you're grown and moved away: they need *to go.*   go someplace else,

at least.   but as he stands there — his cracked back a mikita-crooked blade

in the hoary shoulder-aching dun that cloaks his afternoon's still-sweating
labour — he knows he hasn't yet decided.   hasn't yet decided if this is all

childishness of a kind, or a kind of . . . well, *something else*.   he thinks:

that boy: his boy, his care with everything but what used to really matter.   and then
he remembers, as one often does in basements, with a splinter-stung ferocity,

          that quirk-stilted sort of kinship his boy had had — *still has*, goddammit,

(for all he knows) — with almost all manner of broken things, especially those long past
their time.   that wrong-headed, near-girlish bond with gadgets

          like *this* trash, these old goal sticks — the vics, the sher-woods, even

that goddamn *red* first louisville (from the long-since cobwebbed zeller's, at what used to be
the mall less than 5 minutes from their local rink, from that tim horton's with

          the shorter lines).   and then suddenly he's caught: caught, and right back

there in line.   and so he pauses briefly, frozen in the current of the basement; but
then the moment snaps: a brittle shaft under the torque of this attempt.   he can't,

          he thinks, (or won't) wrap his mind around that superstitious nonsense here

in the new-found echo of his tidied cellar; can't wind the rhetoric quite tight enough
with tape to grasp it firm and hold it closely to himself. he can't, quite simply, make it stick;

          can't negotiate the blade's edge turns of what he imagines must be

that boy's slick strides of thought.   but, even so, he cannot (even here
and now it feels a bit too much like a betrayal, another burial; like ending) throw them out.

          so they've sat here in the dank; been here longer than his boy.   and

now they sit here still, years later, propped against the cracking concrete — the foundation
of this, *his* house — like the old man stooped on a porch he fears

he'll soon become; like a postcardy kitsch of farm implements left to the side

of some barely travelled, rough back road.   but if his phone would ring right now,
he's sure the brittle air would crack — would fracture where he stands.

          he's sure nearly everything would split apart and yaw

like a rambunctious group of kids exploding through rink doors and then
across a fresh and slick new sheet of ice.   if his phone would only ring, he knows

he'd chance to run an open hand along just one of these

old sticks — let its splintering slip through

the failing guard of his ever-thinning skin to draw some blood.

the forecheck

Every pause pauses in its own style.
          — *from* 50-50 Draw *by Don McKay*

a routine dump-and-chase.   and everything, from these seats,
careens right along; strides through each next measure

of the hanging clock's score.   it's a taut, swirling music of legs
churning up ice, until the moment snaps like a neck —

fractures and then droops, like the sudden cracked slack of
your jaw that one night when she paused, over dinner,

as you swallowed a bite, and announced she was leaving;
for good.   now come the gasps, as — from these seats —

all we know is something's — *someone's* — gone airborne and awry; come
down corkscrewed and then stayed a hunched jersey bundle,

all awkwardly still.   it seems there's a pause
while we crane, then a whistle.   at first glance, we can't tell.

          but we try not to wonder to ourselves if he's broken
his neck; whether feeling will sizzle its grudging way back,

sting the hushed tips of fingers or toes.   so instead
we just shuffle our feet in their place — kick

spilt popcorn and wait fretfully through this last stoppage in play.
          and as they cradle his head, hold it frozen in place,

we check wristwatches and programs, even
out-of-town scores, while the goaltender plows his snowed crease, post to

post.   one more mess swept over.   aside, with the rest.

short shifts

a skate's rhetoric
is cruel, cuts to the quick. it
has no mind for still.

    *

the well-held blade; a
wooden ear. a finely grained
listening to what's passed.

    *

puck. the one dark thing
that tears across the gaze, its
edge; our watchful eye.

    *

zamboni's after-
thought — a slickly mirrored dream.
possibility:

             *

each bruise thrums the low
bass ache of disappointment.
         a loss is a loss.

when skates break

                        that ice in its liquid form is solvent
should not confuse matters. this is all about stains;
this game concerns itself with scars. in fact, the surgical

violence of that first step is merely prelude, an introduction;
a perverse baptismal. i remember our knees —
carpet-raw, bloody with tape-ball hockey and too much

sleep-over sugar; rec rooms alive and stale-gear-crowded
with the thrill of an oilers game on tv out east.
and, especially now, years later, after this afternoon's

failure, when the chill anticipation of this october night
has shuddered and cracked — given way like we
imagine our childhood ponds never did, never have —

there is still a sense of tired awe. and the old goalie-skates:
broken, a grade nine remnant now retired, are
propped in the corner, here — their blade acne, their

cracked plastic, become something more than nostalgia;
become a grudging admission of ambiguity. become
a memorial to the resiliency of water in all its states.

the shortest distance, a blue line

there comes a point.   you
find yourself — between straps, between
each wrist-shrugged lace tug and grip;
between any of it and the thing that is
to follow, in the bowels of pre-game or
post. you find yourself getting god awful and
nostalgic.   there. it comes, a point: you
begin to foreshadow your own demise;
realize you're simply breathing life into nothing
more than your own retired back —
story.   and you are reduced, at these
moments, to the cheap, gum-dusted rasp
of your own finger's dry slide across
a hockey carded-version of yourself.   you
know the stats by heart, your fingerprints
the smudging proof.   these are your worst
days.   but then there is the ice.

        a cliché you wake into, all early
morning. each and every, if you could. and
at *these* moments there is no point
to which you'll get. all is well, again.   your
knee bends quick and strong; reactioned.
          but this is not — make no mistake —
redemption; this is no romantic reclamation,
no quaint internal waxing on the necessity
of outdated corner-board ads for long closed
corner stores.   no.   this
is transference, end-of-intermission slick and
simple.   you take your boy's small chill
pink hand: you grab his stick, and
head for the car, already warming in your spot.

shutout

Nothing is exactly equal to anything
             — *from* Sitting *by John Smith*

            truth be told, even the best —
their wallets fat with zeroes — would allow just this:
     that it exists only in the fraction

of the clock's work that borders nineteen-fifty-nine and
twenty, inhabits the cool scintilla between
     zero-zero-one and naught, nothing

at all.   before this, it is nothing but a grand conjecture
— all sweat and blinking and wishful
     thinking; the kindly physics of what the brooding sort

call luck.   afterwards, of course, it's nothing but
a laurel leathered and browning between
          the crisp, pressed sheets of some dim mind's scrapbook.

a score already settled.   but in that
quick-slipped instant, the goal line's rink-rafterward reach
          is a one-way mirror, an unbroken pane

of glass, reflecting.   and this near-transparent
juncture? it is something wholly unspoken and
          unseen; a threshold. everything and nothing all at once.

official fragments —

the referee

> *And the referee?*
> — *from* Hockey Players, *by Al Purdy*

and the referee?   tonight, he's that father: newly unemployed, drunk,
and late.   he can't win; can't quite pick his poison —

he's an unsteady coach still dressing-room blown and rant-reeling, near
trapezing the freshly slicked ice, that slip-kickish and sudden unease.

*

linesman

the older neighbour's younger brother.   or, a bully's sidekick; that one
guy — pointing and waving as you're trying to slip past

and slide away.   your conscience; the niggling presence that wouldn't
let you cheat, that made your hands sweat guilty ink.

*

timekeeper

       try to find him.   you'll see it — in his eyes.
forever in the interim, always waiting . . . for . . .   and yet happy

as a tick.   you see: it's never now with him —
always: *just then* . . .   or: *wait; wait* . . .   a breath; and gone.

      *

the goal judge

believe me — i know this takes no leap of faith
or otherwise, no derring-do.   a goddamn switch gets flicked, some

button thumbed — then the skinner-boxed crowd ignites. delight, i now
understand, is simple reflex; a snap.   a slip of the thumb.

*

dressing room religion

       the zamboni's liquid absolution washed over
the night's early scars and imperfections —
a minor prophet's slow cup of river, or a mother's spittle-

moistened thumb.   and then the bottom strap on
my right goalie pad gave way to my too eager
pre-game tugging; acquiesced to the childlike fervour

a two week layoff and november's night cold
can produce.   but it should not have been a surprise, given
that only moments before there had been a break, a

snag, or disruption in routine.   and at that time my old
watch had reappeared — jumped out from the shadowy
fold and scrum of my gear bag after a year or so.   and

in that one snap of an instant, that moment of
leather's realization of its limits, even the easy give-and-take
of our locker-room banter seemed stilted, measured.   time

became an issue, became concrete, became
a musty, sweat-soaked counting that had clawed its way out of
a bag full of precautions and protections. it showed itself

as resurgent, as lording over everything — even the finest
craftsmanship and tanning that northern ontario could produce.
          so as i struggled with that

loose strip of leather, the rink airhorn's blast immediacy
ringing in my ears, i hoped the old rink clock had blown a fuse
or lost some bulbs.   hoped that the scoreboard had

ceased to function and we would be left to ourselves; left
to our temporary scratching, without
the intrusion of any counting or the tabling of results.

playing hurt

            each shift another gauze-white lie you tell
yourself, a minor falsehood you put on by rote:
one that rarely catches your eye.   but surely,
these fibs to ourselves are the ones we *should* see —
steely eyed — through, if only we'd half-chance;
if we'd bother to take a slow, deep breath and look
up or away from the run of the play — this
odd-manned rush, the drawn glide and slash of
this tumult against which we've tensored ourselves.
            but no: you're now stitched in place.
chin strapped and sewn ragged, but sure, in
a ragtag, frayed-jersey quilt: one you've piece-pinned
together for show.   a necessity, this.
            the cool, dark art of our self-deception: its
grimace-quickening flex against the bruise-new
tightness that seizes this crux in your chest.   but
perhaps, this is all — in the end — for the best,

these half-truths you project on the mirroring
rink.   some would venture a guess it's because
of that twinge you refuse to address, the one
stabbing your strides towards or away — that pang
and its twist you chose to protect— that you
barely, *just barely,* over the course of the game, begin
to see a new sense coalesce; you begin, more or
less, to acknowledge one thing: the cold, blade-thin
line between injured and hurt. *that* subtle difference.

beer & the lazarus eye

       blind.   talk post-game was that i'd got him: the corner of
my blocker: leathered him shut in one eye. that

he'd deserved it.   but blind?   my capacity for violence is almost (most
times) non-existent — save for this, once: that instance: of collision,

of penalty's killing heat and a cool internal streaming. meeting,
like fronts; like systems of weather. acquainting as forces so keen

that they register initially in temperature and only
later explode into the visual, the pupil-yawing destructive, a

lightning.   all that caught me, seized my right
arm, like a feebly constructed barn (by chance girdered and shingled

in place, in the face of an unpredictable storm or other act
of god) and whipped it about and around and damn-near through

that guy's eye after he sticked me, post-whistle.   save
for just that, my record's unblemished, a clean sheet.   but blind?   no.

          later that week in the rinky breath-against-morning
glass haze and sweat of a bar (not hospital, not *cnib*, not cane-handling his way

along and across the length of a street or
park), i saw him: eyes all doubly beer (not coke) bottle thick: his gaze a still

sepia reminder; stigmata.   and he saw me — so
from respective benches we tipped our ills down throats,

swallowed; ate of our icy covenant. nearly held it in dumb hands to see.

backyard rink

— poem for a friend whose grandfather died

        it's like this. each and every night, the hose
more familiar; the water back-slapping
        against the slab as we stand here in the crisp
        dark.   this is, we've tacitly decided,
our best approach.   there's very little
        real speech between us; the air accommodating,
        frigid. our jaws locked against its brace
nearly as stiffly as our knees are scaffolded
        counter to the weeping ice, its slick
        suggestion of missteps.   in fact,
by the time we've once-overed the backyard
        rink, our legs are heavy and damp with this
        effort, the leaking hose and its semblance of
connection all askew.   it's like this,

we've tacitly decided. there's very little but
    the weeping ice; our jaws locked, knees
scaffolded. we've once-overed this,
        stiffly.   each and every night,
    we stand here in the crisp. more familiar;
dark. our effort and missteps, heavy and damp,
        tacitly between us. it's like this: night, all askew.

psalm for an old goalie

with apologies to The Weakerthans

let this ice of ours be one step slower as the game glints and thins towards
       its finish, a blade ground down as rink lights flicker

overhead.   let the last shot's staccato music ricochet and then refract
       more kindly — kindredly pinball through and off

our scrum of ankles and hit him squarely in the chest.   let this
       tiny blackslapped moment stick and rest for one near-frozen clock-tick

and tumble, easy, to his feet.   and then — and *only then* —
       let those anxious knees give way and swoon to smother what it is

he's shouldered for so long.   let each and every thing he reaches for tug
       only slightly at that outstretched glove and then nestle

snugly in his palm, a recollection hinging at his wrist.   let his last breath
        be icy sure and smooth as it whispers clouds around

his cage.   let him know when to hold dear and freeze
        the puck, when to push off, and when to rage against our errant sticks

stabbing at his side.   let him come to understand this
        all, and take it with him where he goes: let him, one last time, glide,

        before the ref whistles goodnight.

the lost art of waving

Local Minor Hockey Coach Loses Fingers in Practice Accident
    — Newspaper Headline

we often leave; less so, we take leave of ourselves, our
senses. get away, we think, *let loose*. think nothing, or little,
of it at the time. but our hands — our volar alter egos — in
these instances: they are an incriminating language: the fingered
diction we slur drunkenly across the widening air, or one
whose rhetoric assumes the form of an urge to blanket a naked palm
against a sheet of ice, its lick; to tempt and toy that nip; make
circus-show with those tiger's teeth of cold. it's a paradox, really.
heat, almost — this crystalline itch, this close cousin of a wave. but
we all know something of it, as does our kneeling, puck-collecting,
peewee coach. (let's call him al, or steve, or mr. gardner.)
in one manner or another, we have felt that very same sort of
whisper chill up and suggest itself: *escape*.   but right now

we're safe and stuck at home, the paper strewn across the table, and
it's a headline, and only a headline we thumb across — albeit
a pretty small one — buried in the briefs beside the box scores.
framed there, it reminds us of the hazard of departure in its purest
form, of forgetting ourselves too much.   so as we pull back
from the page, licking the inked grey bruise of this knowledge from
our tingling hands, all injured-animal motion — we can almost
taste it. fire, at first, comes to mind. that, and the glowing ends of
things: cigarettes from a distance at night; ballpark red hots too
long for their buns. and then we see what we imagine might be his
(our daring coach's) hand — a sudden splayed book of matches —
fingers tip-sparked and scintillating warm; sanguine flames glaring
against the now blooming flint of the ice.   and he looks
up.   (we imagine he *must have* looked up, just as
we now do — up and away from the stark text of the incident,
his incident. think *perhaps he's done it:* left it, us included, all
behind.)   but the skate blade (that glint instant of escape)

is gone, and the ligature of disbelief — what he's now left
with — is no match for the still-spilling heat that leaks from his
hand. floodlight-on-steel suddenly, quick as the stitch of a
needle's last dip past zero, he's lost it, our coach. slipped it, *let* it
slip — from the severed tips of his fingers. this is escape, altogether
unexpected.   and us? we rub our own hands together
here, at the table, convincing ourselves that something, once
written down — whatever it is we read — is always a kind of
fiction, escapable, able to be left behind; we grab onto — holding tight
— the fluttering, papery-thin weight of our conviction that's so.

Acknowledgements / Notes on the poems

The writing of these poems was generously supported by the New Brunswick Arts Board through a grant from their Emerging Artists Program.

Not surprisingly, given free agency, some of the poems in this collection have taken shifts over the course of their careers wearing the sweaters of the following publications and anthologies: *Aethlon: Journal of Sports Literature*, *The Antigonish Review*, *Arc*, *Denver Quarterly*, *Desire*, *Doom & Vice: a Canadian Collection*, *Diagram*, *Exact Fare Only 2*, *Event*, *4am*, *Geist*, *Indiana Review*, *Literature: A Pocket Anthology*, *The New Quarterly*, *Poetry: A Pocket Anthology*, *Pottersfield Portfolio*, *Prairie Fire*, *Prism International*, *(Some From) Diagram: Selections from the Magazine and More* and *Zygote*.

An earlier version of "the lost art of waving" was originally written and performed for CBC Radio's Poetry Face-Off.

A vintage version of "to montreal, by bus, for the game" has appeared on CBC Radio 3's website: www.cbcradio3.com.

A version of "how we keep it together" was chosen as the 2nd place winner of *Arc* magazine's 2004 *Poem of the Year Contest* and appeared in the magazine and on their website as a result.

The poem "splinter" owes an assist to an earlier poem about old hockey sticks entitled "practice:" that appeared in *how we play at it: a list* (ECW Press, 2002).

A few 'third jersey,' alternate versions of a number of the poems in this collection appeared in a limited edition, letter-pressed chapbook titled *tracery & interplay* (Frog Hollow Press, 2004). Thanks are due to Caryl Peters and the press for their dedication to poetry and fine printing. You can visit Frog Hollow Press at: www.froghollowpress.com.

Thanks to James Arthur for his insightful comments on many of these poems and for his suggestion of possible titles for the entire collection, as well as to Michael Holmes for his meticulous editing. Thanks, too, to the members of the 2004-05 UNB Intramural League Champion UNB *Law Litigators* hockey team for providing on-ice inspiration for these poems. And thanks, of course, to Marissa, who suffers through version after version of poem after poem as I play them through the process.

About the Author

matt robinson works in Residential Life at The University of New Brunswick in Fredericton, where he also plays goal in the UNB Intramural Hockey League (for the 2004-05 League Champion UNB *Law Litigators*).

A two-time National Magazine Award finalist, robinson's poetry has received numerous awards, including The Petra Kenney International Poetry Prize and *Grain's* Prose Poem Prize. A recipient of The NB Foundation for the Arts' Emerging Artist of the Year Award, his poems have appeared on radio and television, in numerous Canadian, American, British, and Australian publications, as well as in anthologies such as *Breathing Fire 2* (Nightwood, 2004), *Poetry: A Pocket Anthology* (Pearson, 2004), *Literature: A Pocket Anthology* (Pearson, 2004), *Coastlines: The Poetry of Atlantic Canada* (Goose Lane, 2002), *Exact Fare Only 2* (Anvil, 2004), and *Landmarks* (Acorn Press, 2001). A poetry editor at *The Fiddlehead*, robinson has also served as NB / PEI Regional Rep and President of The League of Canadian Poets.

robinson's previous books of poetry include the letter-pressed, limited edition chapbook of hockey poems, *tracery & interplay* (Frog Hollow Press, 2004), as well as the full-length collections *how we play at it: a list* (ECW Press, 2002), and *A Ruckus of Awkward Stacking* (Insomniac, 2000), which was short-listed for both the Gerald Lampert Memorial and ReLit Poetry Awards.